TU___S

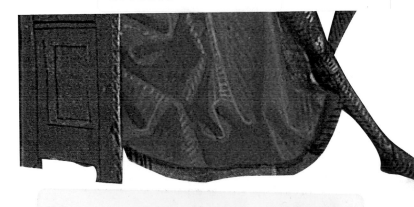

CONTENTS

COUNTRY LIFE

Most country households brewed their own wine, beer or cider. Any excess was transported to nearby towns in barrels on packhorses.

*W*hile poorer people still farmed strips of land in large, open fields and paid a tythe, or rent, to the church or local lord who owned the land, a new breed of farmer was emerging, called yeomen. They rented or bought several fields together to form small farms, usually on the outskirts of the village, and built themselves fine houses. They also employed labourers from the village to tend the fields instead of working on the land themselves and formed a 'middle class' of landowner, not so wealthy as the lords but much better off than the peasants.

WORKING THE LAND

Despite the growth of towns in both size and number, about 90% of the population still earned their living from the land.

NATURAL CYCLES

Country life was dictated by natural cycles; by the seasons, the weather and the available daylight hours. Specific agricultural tasks had to be performed at certain times of the year. Here, peasants are pruning vines, usually undertaken each March.

4

OFF TO MARKET

Every town of any size held a weekly market, where people from the surrounding villages came to sell their wares and buy any goods not available locally. Poultry, butter, eggs, cheese, grain, fish and livestock were all sold at markets which, like fairs, became great social gatherings.

DOMESTIC COMFORTS

Life in the countryside was simple, but there was a growing level of sophistication as the country as a whole began to feel the benefits of increased foreign trade and travel. Domestic comforts increased as the quality of houses improved and higher wages meant that more people could eat healthier. Some could now afford meat and vegetables to add variety to their meagre diets. This picture shows a fish and sausage being grilled. The illustration on the right is a leather water bucket.

VILLAGE LIFE

Village life had changed little since the Middle Ages. Most people did not venture far from home as villages were often self-contained. Villages had their own windmill to grind corn and local tradesmen making and selling goods not produced by the villagers themselves.

LIFE IN TOWNS

Improved methods of agriculture meant that fewer people were needed to work the land. Many peasants were evicted from their homes when their fields were sold off or turned over to sheep pasture for the rapidly expanding wool trade. The majority moved into towns to seek work as labourers for the growing number of merchants and traders who set up business there as a result of increased foreign trade. These changes occurred fairly quickly which meant overcrowding was a problem. Many of the houses were of inferior quality and crammed into narrow streets. Sanitation was poor and there were frequent outbreaks of disease, such as plague and cholera.

FRESH WATER

Fresh drinking water in towns was difficult to obtain. Most people bought their supplies from water-carriers, who transported water in from the country.

READ ALL ABOUT IT

Following the introduction of coffee into England from South America it quickly became a very fashionable, though expensive drink. Rich people met at 'coffee houses' in towns to exchange views and read newspapers (introduced in 1622 but only available in limited editions) or political pamphlets.

FIRE

One of the biggest risks in towns was fire. Most of the buildings were made of wood and thatch, allowing the flames to spread easily. The Great Fire of London started on 2nd September 1666. It raged for five days unchecked, killing nine people and destroying over 13,000 buildings.

LIFE FOR THE RICH

FUNERAL HELM

Although changing methods of warfare had made armour an unnecessary encumbrance, many noblemen still owned a suit of elaborately decorated ceremonial armour, which they might wear at court or, as in this case, at their own funeral.

By contrast, many people already comfortably off became very wealthy indeed, mostly as a result of increased foreign trade and exploitation as England began to extend its empire. With a strong government at home, many nobles replaced their austere castles with magnificent mansions, sparing no expense on the decorations and furnishings, or on their personal vanity, spending vast amounts of money on clothes and jewellery.

A COVER UP

To counteract the often unpleasant smells encountered around the house, or town, wealthy Tudor women carried a pomander, or scent bottle, on their belt. This silver-gilt example dates from c.1580 and had four separate compartments for different aromatic perfumes.

A LOVETOKEN

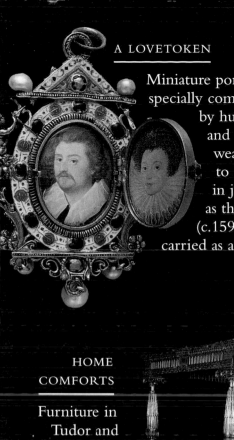

Miniature portraits were
specially commissioned
by husbands
and wives from
wealthy families
to be inserted
in jewellery, such
as this gold locket
(c.1590), and
carried as a love token.

OLD BEFORE THEIR TIME

This painting of the Saltonstall family shows
clearly the fashion for wealthy parents to
dress children as young adults as soon as they
were out of baby clothes.

HOME COMFORTS

Furniture in
Tudor and
Stuart noble
households
became
ever more
elaborate and
comfortable,
typified by
this exquisitely
carved four-poster bed.
Curtains could be lowered for
privacy and warmth.

ART FOR ART'S SAKE

With the opening up of
the seaways in the 16th
and 17th centuries vast
fortunes were made, allowing
the rich to adorn their houses
with works of art. This elaborate,
though impractical, 'Nautilus
Cup' (c.1585) is made of
silver gilt and shell.

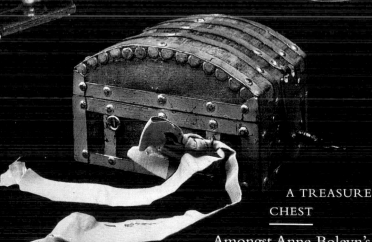

A TREASURE CHEST

Amongst Anne Boleyn's
(Henry VIII's second wife) most
treasured possessions was her jewellery, which she carried with
her on her frequent royal processions in this charming casket.

THE POOR AT HOME

It is estimated that in the 16th and 17th centuries about half the population lived in poverty. Many resorted to begging, although it was illegal and they might be punished, or even hanged, if caught. Eventually, almshouses (similar to workhouses) were set up to help the poor, elderly and infirm who could no longer support themselves.

TRADITIONAL ROLES

Traditionally, men and women in the poorer households all had to work and had their own specific responsibilities. The roles were clearly defined, the men working mostly in the fields and tending the livestock, while the women did the housework, cooked and made clothes. At busy times, such as harvesting, women would also be expected to help their husbands on the land.

SUBSISTENCE LIVING

The poor often led a subsistence (or minimal) standard of living. Many still farmed the communal strips of land on the outskirts of the villages and kept a few chickens to supplement their income by selling the eggs. The husband and wife in this illustration are chasing away a fox about to kill one of their chickens.

ARE YOU SITTING COMFORTABLY?

Furniture was basic in poor households, usually consisting of a trestle table and bench seats. The suckling pig in the middle of the table indicates this is a special occasion.

MEALTIMES

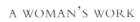

Only the well-off could afford pewter tableware, the poor had to content themselves with earthenware, often made by the householders themselves. This clay jug is typical and dates from about 1550–1600.

IN THE NURSERY

One of the principal duties for women in the poorer households was looking after the children.

Here, a mother is seen nursing a baby, with an older child alongside in a wooden pram.

A WOMAN'S WORK

Women also tended the poultry yard and carried out dairying tasks, including the production of milk, butter and cheese. Traditionally, they took their own excess produce to market and were allowed to keep the proceeds to spend as they wished.

FOOD AND DRINK

The rich ate well with a wide variety of meats and vegetables regularly on the menu, including potatoes, recently introduced from America but still very expensive. Poorer classes had a more restricted diet of dairy produce, bread, basic vegetables and occasionally meat, such as rabbit. The rich drank wine at table, while the poor drank ale. Food was preserved in spices, or salt, though there were experiments with ice as a preservative by the late 17th century.

A DELICACY

While we might frown upon it now, swans were considered a great delicacy for the rich. Poorer classes might content themselves with goose.

FOOD DISPENSER

This fine piece of tableware is a Tudor peppermill recovered from the 'Mary Rose'.

TABLE SERVICE

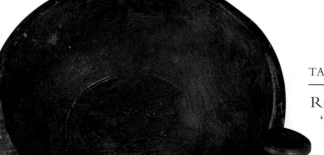

Retrieved from the wreck of the 'Mary Rose' this impressive collection of tableware shows the general level of sophistication practised at table by early Tudor times. The dishes and plates are of pewter, or wood.

TABLE MANNERS

The children of Lord Cobham seated around the table are eating a variety of fresh fruits – with their pets wandering amongst the food !

HARE TODAY, GAME TOMORROW

Hare and game birds, such as pheasant or partridge, were common additions to the rich man's table, while rabbits, caught wild, might supplement the poor man's diet.

FOOD PREPARATION

The kitchen at Hampton Court shows how food was prepared (usually on wooden surfaces) in the 16th and 17th centuries. Cooking was still done mostly on open fires.

'GIN LANE'

Alcohol was cheap and excessive drinking amongst the poor, to ease the misery of poverty, became a problem, as this engraving by Hogarth shows.

IMPROVING THE FLAVOUR

To improve the flavour of game, such as pheasant, deer and rabbit, it was hung in a cold room for several days before eating. Although still practised today, meat was then left until maggot-ridden to sweeten the taste.

13

PASTIMES

Although people worked long hours, there were a lot of 'holy-days' (holidays) throughout the year when no-one was expected to work. People played a variety of games (for fun rather than as organised sports) such as hockey, cricket and football. The latter was played with a pig's bladder for a ball and was very different from today's game. Two teams from neighbouring villages met somewhere between the two communities. The object was to get the ball back to your own village - any way you could !

The theatre was popular, though women were not allowed to act, young boys taking women's roles.

HITTING THE RIGHT NOTE

For people of all classes music has always played a prominent role as a source of entertainment, with professional musicians providing the music at court and dances. The Tudor period, however, saw the growth of individuals learning to play an instrument, or singing, for their own amusement.

TREADING THE BOARDS

This picture shows the reconstructed open-air 'Globe Theatre'. The original was built in 1598-9 and was the most popular theatre in London. Shakespeare owned an eighth share in it and staged many of his plays there.

THE BARD OF AVON

William Shakespeare (1564-1616), perhaps the best-known and greatest English dramatist, began his career, first as a stage hand in the Elizabethan theatre, then as an actor before going on to write plays.

THE HUNT

Hawking and hunting remained popular pastimes throughout the Tudor and Stuart periods. Deer were the most popular quarry, but wild boar and wolves still roamed the countryside then and were considered fair game.

BLOOD SPORTS

Bear-baiting, where dogs were set upon a tethered bear and bets made on the outcome, was a popular though cruel blood sport.

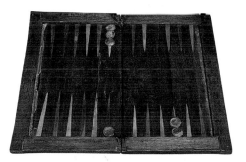

BOARD GAMES

Board games were popular indoor pastimes. This backgammon board (known as tables) was found aboard the 'Mary Rose'.

COMING UP TRUMPS

Card games were popular, both for pleasure and for gambling. The four players here are playing primero, an early forerunner of poker. The modern card pack is still based on Elizabethan court dress.

FASHION

LUCKY CHARM

Pendants, such as this one worn by Elizabeth I, were believed to be lucky charms to ward off evil and ill-health.

ashion trends were greatly influenced by the monarch and court. The rich spent a lot of money on clothes. Elizabeth I had 260 gowns, 99 robes, 127 cloaks, 125 petticoats and hundreds of smaller accessories in her wardrobe. For the poor, coarse woollen clothes had to suffice, dyed one colour using vegetable dyes. But for the rich a range of materials was available, including linen and silk, which could be dyed or printed in a variety of colours and often richly embroidered. Women wore loose ruffs, while men exaggerated their stature by wearing huge, padded shoulders.

LAYER UPON LAYER

Clothes for men were built up in layers for extra warmth. The nobleman in this picture wears leggings beneath a short tunic, with an inner and an outer cloak of ermine-lined red velvet.

FINE JEWELS

Both men and women wore exquisite jewellery. Many fine jewels were imported with the opening up of new trade routes, such as this late-Medieval necklace from Russia.

THE VIRGIN QUEEN (1558–1603)

Elizabeth I, daughter of Henry VIII by his second wife, Ann Boleyn, was ever conscious of being a woman in a male-dominated world. She was very particular about her appearance and is said to have taken a bath (then considered unwholesome) four times a year whether she needed it or not !

BLACK TEETH

Many Tudor people had rotten teeth. However, one of the more unusual fashions of the time was the practice of deliberately blacking-out the front teeth, particularly among noble women. The practice may have developed to disguise genuinely rotten teeth.

IF YOU CAN'T STAND THE HEAT

To disguise the pock scars of smallpox, candle wax was smoothed into the skin. The wax tended to melt if it came too close to the fire !

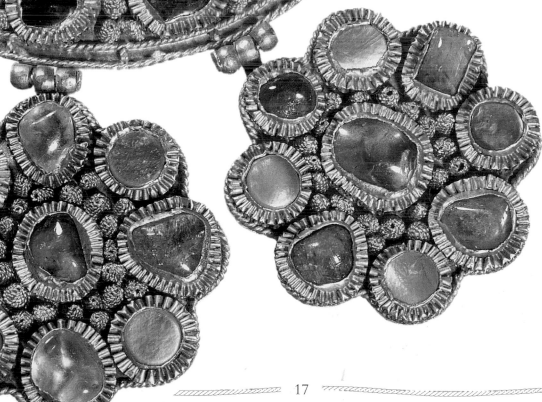

ART AND ARCHITECTURE

Great houses were usually built in brick, making them warmer and much more welcoming than their stone Medieval counterparts had been, with more attention paid to comfort and large windows to admit extra light. In the 17th century a Renaissance took place, with artists and architects reaching back to classical Rome for their inspiration. Gothic ideals were rejected in favour of the rounded arches and domes of buildings such as St. Paul's Cathedral in London, rebuilt by Sir Christopher Wren after the Medieval cathedral had been destroyed in the Great Fire of 1666.

SUMPTUOUS INTERIORS

With the advent of more settled times, more money could be spent on the interior comforts of castles and houses rather than on defensive features.

CHANGING STYLES

Ightham Mote, an unfortified manor house in Kent, preserves a delightful blend of Medieval, Tudor and Jacobean domestic features.

RED-BRICK MANSION

Originally begun in 1515 by Cardinal Wolsey and given by him to Henry VIII, Hampton Court has been greatly extended by successive monarchs. It is a magnificent, luxuriously decorated palace with no defensive features whatsoever.

LONG LIVE THE KING

This enigmatic oil painting of the Coronation Procession of Charles II in 1660
(by Dirck Stoop) shows an early and imaginative use of perspective.

FURNITURE AS ART

This elaborately carved case
is made from imported
black ebony wood.
Each panel contains
a miniature painting
and bust.

EVERY PICTURE
TELLS A STORY

Portraiture first came to
prominence under the Tudors.
This study of Edward VI, by
an unknown artist, is typical of
the period. Tudor artists tried to
capture the expression of
feeling by visual impression.
By contrast with Medieval
paintings, which were
more symbolic, Tudor
works are more austere
and attempt to
flatter their
subjects.

HEALTH AND MEDICINE

CRUEL TO BE KIND

Although it looks like he is being tortured, this patient is having a brain operation, without an anaesthetic.

There were frequent outbreaks of bubonic plague. The culprit was a species of flea, carried by rats aboard ships coming from the Middle East. Over 100,000 Londoners died in the 1665 outbreak alone. Diseases, especially epidemics such as the plague or cholera, were seen as divine punishment from God and magical remedies still featured strongly in any treatment to rid the patient of evil. Important breakthroughs in understanding human anatomy were made in the 17th century when the Church finally allowed dead bodies to be used for research.

GREENWICH HOSPITAL

Greenwich Hospital stands on the site of the Tudor palace of Placentia, birthplace of Henry VIII and Elizabeth I. It was rebuilt by Charles II, to designs by Sir Christopher Wren, and again by William III and Mary II. Mary founded the hospital in 1694 by Royal Charter, converting the unfinished palace buildings for the purpose. In 1873 the buildings were again converted for use as the Royal Naval College.

BUBONIC PLAGUE

The popular children's rhyme: 'Ring-a-ring-o' roses, A pocketful of posies, Atishoo, atishoo, We all fall down', alludes to the plague. Garlands of herbs were carried to ward off the disease and sneezing was one of the early symptoms. Death usually followed within just five days. The hand bell was rung by undertakers who collected the dead.

A MODERN EVIL

Although Sir John Hawkins introduced tobacco into England (from the American colonies in 1565) it is Sir Walter Raleigh who made smoking fashionable. It was smoked in clay pipes and by the early 17th century there were 7000 shops selling tobacco in London alone. Today about one in four smokers dies from diseases directly caused by smoking.

LIFE EXPECTANCY

This picture shows the five ages of man – baby, youth, adult, old age and finally death. Child mortality was high, over half of those born dying in their first year. Only one person in ten was expected to reach 40.

LOVE AND MARRIAGE

For most people marriage was more a matter of convenience than love. Many noblemen arranged the marriages of their children (particularly girls, who might be married as young as 12) in order to make political or monetary alliances. For the poorer classes it was often simply a matter of economics, girls looking for any man of prospects who might be able to support them. When Charles II came back to the throne in 1660, following 11 years of repressive Puritan rule, a sexual revolution swept the land with the result that many inhibitions were dropped.

COURTSHIP RITUALS

Young suitors of noble birth called upon their ladies at court (from where the modern word courtship derives) and conducted their romances under the supervision of chaperones.

VOWS OF CHASTITY

Everyone entering into marriage took vows of chastity, but some husbands, particularly lords away at court, took them very seriously indeed. They made their wives wear a chastity belt to ensure they remained faithful, though they were free of course to do as they wished !

MARRIAGE FEAST

This painting of a marriage feast at Bermondsey about 1569 gives a good impression of an Elizabethan society wedding. Festivities could go on for several days.

THE OLDEST PROFESSION

Women who fell on hard times, for example those widowed young and thus deprived of an income, might have to resort to prostitution. This woodcut (c.1600) shows men gambling in an Elizabethan brothel.

A ROVING EYE

Charles II (the 'Merry Monarch') was invited by Parliament to become king in 1660. As part of the bargain Charles had to marry Catherine of Braganza, from Portugal. It was a loveless marriage and he had many mistresses, including the actress Nell Gwynn, pictured here.

WOMEN AND CHILDREN

Tudor and Stuart England was very much a male dominated society in which women and children had few rights. Wives were expected to obey their husbands and if they did not, or if they nagged, they might face the ducking stool as a punishment. Women were expected to help out in the fields, cook, keep house and mind the children. The only real profession open to them was nursing. Only children from wealthy families went to school, and then usually just the boys.

CHILD'S PLAY

Although poorer children started work as young as six to help support the family, there was time to play. This toy gun is made of wood and is an authentic reproduction of a hand pistol.

HORN BOOK

Children were taught to read using a simple horn book. A piece of paper, mounted on a wooden board, was covered by a thin sheet of transparent horn as protection.

ALL IN A DAY'S WORK

This 17th century cottage interior shows a mother and grandmother carrying out cooking and laundry duties, while a child learns to walk in a wheeled baby walker.

FUN AND GAMES

The boys in this picture (from a well-off family judging by the clothes) are playing a form of hop-scotch.

'BLOODY' MARY

Although Princess Mary was the first of Henry VIII's children to survive, women had few rights and succession to the throne was considered unseemly. She only succeeded to the throne following the death of Edward VI, her half-brother. She was a Catholic and had over 300 people executed for refusing to revert to Catholicism.

A WOMAN'S LOT

Midwifery was one of the few professions open to women. Note the surgical instruments on the belt of the seated woman. The men in the background are calculating the astrological chart for the new baby.

ORPHANS

Orphaned children had no rights whatsoever. For the lucky ones special courts appointed guardians, but many became vagabonds, relying on church charity for food.

A TRAGIC AFFAIR

Lady Jane Grey was the cousin and childhood sweetheart of Edward VI. When he realised he was dying, he decided that she should rule after his death instead of his half-sister, Mary. She came to the throne at 16 and ruled for just nine days, before relinquishing the crown to Mary. She was later beheaded for treason.

WAR AND WEAPONRY

'MONS MEG'

This huge bombard, weighing over 8 tonnes, could fire a stone cannon ball a distance of nearly two miles.

The Wars of the Roses were civil wars between the rival families of York and Lancaster, each claiming the English throne. Richard III lost his crown to Henry Tudor (House of Lancaster) who as Henry VII became the first Tudor monarch in 1485. When Henry VIII split with the Church of Rome he incurred the wrath of the Pope and lived under constant threat of invasion. Relations with Spain worsened in Elizabeth's reign when a massive armada was sent against England in 1588, which was routed by Sir Francis Drake. Charles I's attempt to rule without Parliament resulted in another Civil War (1642-46). He eventually lost the cause and was beheaded in 1649.

HUMILIATING DEFEAT

In the 17th century England was frequently at war with Holland. Between 9-14th June 1667 the Dutch inflicted a humiliating defeat on the English navy by sailing up the River Medway, in Kent, and destroying many ships in the fleet.

KEEPING UP APPEARANCES

By the 16th and 17th centuries, with the development of guns, fighting armour was comparatively light, often consisting of breastplates and helmets only. Armour, such as this suit, harkened back to the middle ages and was more ceremonial than practical, used mostly for tournaments.

THE ROUTE OF THE ARMADA

Following their famous defeat in August 1588 the Spanish Armada took flight northwards, around the coast of Scotland. Of 130 ships, only 70 returned home to Spain.

CIVIL WAR

Oliver Cromwell was a farmer before joining the Puritan army. He led the Parliamentarians against the Royalists in the Civil War (1642–49) of Charles I's reign. The king was beheaded in 1649 and England became a republic under Cromwell.

YEOMEN OF THE GUARD

Following Henry VII's victory at Bosworth Field in 1485 several attempts were made on his life. As a precaution, he established a personal bodyguard unit of yeomen at the Tower of London. Their successors still wear the same scarlet uniforms today.

CRIME AND PUNISHMENT

The increased trade and improved agricultural methods, as well as bringing prosperity to some, also created a crime wave from those whose livelihoods were threatened. The population rose, but fewer people were required to work the land. Many landlords turned peasants out of their homes, converting their fields and common lands into sheep pasture. It is estimated that by 1560 there were more than 10,000 homeless people wandering the countryside looking for work. Many resorted to begging, while others turned to crime, even though harsh punishments were introduced to curb the trend.

FLOGGING

Flogging was a common punishment for a number of minor offences, such as stealing, or even simply being caught begging.

HENRY VIII'S IRON RULE

When Henry VIII divorced his first wife, Catherine of Aragon, and broke from the Church of Rome, there was the constant threat of rebellion. He ruled the land with an iron fist and is estimated to have executed several thousand people (though no accurate records exist) mostly because of their religious or political beliefs.

A SENSE OF JUSTICE

Taxation was high and punishments severe. Most towns had a court where Justices of the Peace, who travelled the land, heard criminal cases, but they were unpaid and therefore open to corruption.

Royal prisoners who had been condemned to death, reserved the right to be beheaded by an executioner using a sword, instead of an axe, as it was considered more dignified. Anne Boleyn chose this method at her execution in 1536.

OFF WITH THEIR HEADS

The block and axe was usually reserved for nobility and political prisoners for crimes against the Crown. Victims knelt before the block, with arms outstretched, but the axe was seldom sharp enough to sever the head with one blow.

DEATH BY STONING

Adulterers, or those committing 'crimes' against the Church, were sometimes executed by stoning, or by crushing, having heavy stones piled onto their chests.

TRANSPORT AND SCIENCE

Travel was very difficult, and dangerous, throughout the 16th and 17th centuries. Some of the main roads had metalled surfaces, but most were little more than beaten earth, which became very muddy and impassable in winter months. Most people walked or went on horseback because carriages were still very uncomfortable. In towns, the rich were conveyed in Sedan chairs, similar to a small carriage but with handrails instead of wheels, carried by two men. Toll roads were introduced in 1663 to raise money to improve the roads. The 17th century saw many important new discoveries in the field of science, including research into human anatomy by William Harvey and into physics and gravity by Sir Isaac Newton.

HEARTS OF OAK

English shipwrights became world leaders in designing ships to carry cannon, helping seafarers like Drake, Raleigh and Frobisher to gain supremacy of the open seas. Many were built at the royal dockyards of Chatham and Woolwich, where there was an abundant supply of trees. The oak forests of Kent and Sussex were not cleared to provide the timber, but carefully managed as a crop.

HIDDEN WORLDS

With the invention of the microscope, scientists could see tiny creatures and organisms, such as this flea, scarcely visible to the human eye, for the first time in dazzling detail.

THE SORCERER'S APPRENTICE

Alchemists believed they could transform base metals into gold and, although unsuccessful, they advanced the study of chemistry considerably, particularly in medicine.

This late 17th century compound microscope is similar to one used by the eminent physicist Robert Hooke. For the first time microscopic creatures, too small to be seen with the human eye, could be observed.

IT'S IN THE STARS

Instruments such as this brass astronomical compendium, made in 1569, were used for accurate navigation. They were also used to make astrological charts, which were taken very seriously.

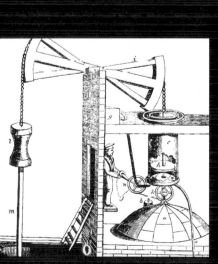

DAWNING OF A NEW AGE

It is not generally acknowledged that the Stuart period marked the beginning of the modern industrial age. This atmospheric engine, used to pump water from mines, was developed by Newcomen and dates from 1705.

RELIGION

The 16th and 17th centuries were periods of great upheaval and reform in the Church. There was already a growing number of people who objected (Protestants) to the Catholic faith before Henry VIII's break with Rome. When Henry failed to get a divorce from Catherine of Aragon by the Pope he established a separate Church of England with himself as head though he remained a staunch Catholic throughout his life. The Protestants rallied to the new Church, which eventually became accepted as a Protestant faith.

CHURCH REFORMS

Pilgrimages to religious shrines were outlawed by the 17th century church reformers who stripped them from the churches.

PURITAN REFORMS

Following the Reformation of the Church by the Tudors, most church decoration, such as this colourful triptych (altar piece) was removed by the Puritans.

A FAIR TRIAL?

Anyone accused of witchcraft was ducked under water. If they drowned, they were considered innocent, but if they survived they were deemed to be a witch and subsequently executed !

DISSOLUTION OF THE MONASTERIES

Following alleged corruption within the monasteries (but more likely as an excuse to seize their wealth) Henry VIII closed them down between 1536-40.

THE GUNPOWDER PLOT

A group of Catholic conspirators, aided by Guido (Guy) Fawkes, an explosives expert, tried unsuccessfully to blow up Parliament and the Protestant James I.

THE FIRST ENGLISH BIBLE

The Catholic missal was replaced by the first English Book of Common Prayer in 1549, following Henry VIII's break with the Church of Rome.

CARDINAL WOLSEY (1475–1530)

Cardinal Wolsey enjoyed a meteoric rise to fame and fortune as Henry VIII's Lord Chancellor. He fell out of royal favour, however, when he failed to secure Henry's divorce from Catherine of Aragon. He was arrested and ordered to the Tower of London for trial, but he died en route.

THE YOUNG HENRY

*H*enry came to the throne at the age of 17, a handsome, robust giant of a man standing 6ft (1.83metres) tall, when the average height was just 5ft. 4ins (1.6metres). He had not been groomed for kingship and lacked the necessary discipline to rule responsibly. A flamboyant character, he squandered his father's fortune and was more interested in sports, music and dancing than in politics, leaving policy-making decisions to a group of astutely chosen ministers.

CEREMONIAL ARMOUR

This finely silvered and engraved suit of armour was made for Henry. It was used mostly for parading during tournaments.

THE THRILL OF THE HUNT

Henry loved to hunt in the forests attached to the royal palaces, particularly with birds of prey. There was a strict hierarchy to be observed, kestrels such as this were flown by lesser nobles, or Henry himself when learning his skills. Later, he would probably have flown a larger species, such as the Peregrine falcon or an eagle.

HENRY VIII

This portrait miniature shows Prince Henry as a young boy. The third child (and second son) of Henry VII, he was not born to rule and only came to the throne as the result of his brother Arthur's untimely death in 1502.

HENRY VII

Henry Tudor was born at Pembroke Castle in 1457. An only child, his mother was the great-great-granddaughter of Edward III. He spent 14 years in exile before being crowned king at the age of 28, beginning the reign of the Tudors.

EVENTS OF HENRY'S LIFE

~1485 22ND AUGUST~
Battle of Bosworth Field

~29TH OCTOBER~
Henry VII crowned

16TH DECEMBER
Catherine of Aragon born

~1486~
Prince Arthur born

~1491 28TH JUNE~
Prince Henry (later Henry VIII) born

~1501 14TH NOVEMBER~
Marriage of Prince Arthur and Catherine of Aragon

~1502~
Prince Arthur dies. Anne Boleyn born

THE TUDORS COME TO POWER

Henry Tudor wrested the crown by defeating the Plantagenet king, Richard III, at the Battle of Bosworth on 22nd August 1485. Civil war (the Wars of the Roses) had raged for over 30 years between two rival claimants to the throne – the House of York (Richard) and the House of Lancaster (Henry).

THE GOLDEN YEARS

The 'Golden Years' of Henry's reign coincided with his marriage to Catherine of Aragon. He married the last five of his wives and committed most of his acts of tyranny within the last third of his reign. When he ascended the throne as a robust, gallant teenager, he was welcomed. The people rejoiced as the years of restraint under Henry VII ended. Henry VIII appeared to promise much, but he did not live up to their expectations.

SEAL OF APPROVAL

Henry VIII's Great Seal, which was stamped onto all official royal documents, including the numerous death warrants issued against his enemies.

THE KING'S DEPARTURE

The scene at Dover, May 1520, when Henry and his court of 5,800 embarked for their meeting with the King of France.

THE 'UNKNOWN WARRIOR'

Henry was very proficient at jousting. He sometimes fought as an unknown contender, only to later reveal his true identity as the victor to the jubilant crowds, who no doubt pretended to be fooled!

THE KING'S GREAT MATTER

Henry blamed Catherine's inability to conceive a son and heir on God's punishment for marrying his brother's widow. He tried to have the marriage annulled on the grounds that it was unlawful, so he could remarry.

COUNTRY RETREAT

The Tudor banqueting hall of Leeds Castle, Kent. Henry built a fine suite of royal apartments here for use when he wished to escape the ills of London.

bascinet

visor

pauldron

breastplate

upper cannon of vambrace

gauntlet

couter

lower cannon of vambrace

tonlet

THE NAMING OF PARTS

cuisse

This suit of armour (and tournament sword) was assembled for Henry in Greenwich c.1520 when he was still a young man of slim stature.

poleyn

greave

sabaton

~1509 22ND APRIL~
Henry VII dies

~11TH JUNE~
Henry marries Catherine of Aragon

~1511 1ST JANUARY~
Prince Henry born

~FEBRUARY~
Prince Henry dies

~1513~
Edmund de la Pole executed

~16TH AUGUST~
Battle of Spurs

~9TH SEPTEMBER~
Battle of Flodden Field

~1516 18TH FEBRUARY~
Princess Mary born

CATHERINE OF ARAGON

BORN
1485

MARRIED
1509

DIVORCED
1533

DIED
1536

Catherine was the only child of King Ferdinand of Spain. She was beautiful, intelligent and fun-loving. For nearly 20 years she and Henry made the perfect royal couple. She bore several children, but only Mary survived. Henry sought to have their marriage annulled, saying it was an unlawful union. The matter eventually led to the break with the Church of Rome. The divorce was finalised in 1533 and Catherine was banished from court. She died alone on 7th January 1536; a sad end to a glittering reign.

THE LAST PAPAL LEGATE

The seal of Cardinal Lorenzo Campeggio (the last papal legate to officiate in England). He referred Henry's application for an annulment directly to the Pope.

BORN TO BE QUEEN

Catherine was betrothed to Prince Arthur when only three to form an Anglo-Spanish alliance. They married in 1501 but within six months she was widowed. She was afterwards betrothed to Henry, who had always liked her, and when they married in 1509 it was out of genuine love.

CATHERINE'S DEFENCE

After much deliberation Catherine's, tribunal in front of the cardinals to contest Henry's application for a divorce, began on 18th June 1529. She argued convincingly that her marriage to Arthur was unconsummated so her union with Henry must be legal.

PERSONAL HYGIENE

Catherine was very particular about her personal hygiene. This very comfortable bathroom, with its fire and linen-lined tub, is very typical of those in the royal palaces.

EVENTS OF HENRY'S LIFE

~1518 3RD OCTOBER~
Treaty of London signed

~1520 7TH JUNE~
'Field of the Cloth of Gold' begins

~1521 11TH OCTOBER~
Henry earns title 'Defender of the Faith'

CATHERINE'S MISSAL

Catherine was devoutly religious and had her own personal missal, richly bound in leather, which she took to mass to follow the prayers.

PRINCESS MARY

Mary was the only child of Catherine and Henry to survive. Born on 18th February 1516 she was largely ignored by Henry after his divorce from Catherine, when her rights to the throne were nullified by Parliament. She was later crowned queen as Mary I in 1553.

PATRON OF THE ARTS

Although usually regarded as a strong, powerful leader, not to say tyrannical in the latter years of his reign, Henry VIII had a gentler side to his nature. He was something of a patron of the arts. He liked to surround himself with beautiful objects and commissioned many paintings, statues and wood carvings. He furnished his many palaces sumptuously and acquired many exquisite pieces of jewellery and fine art, such as clocks. Hans Holbein, a German portrait painter, was employed to record the royal family for posterity. Henry set a precedent, and something of a new fashion at court, by composing musical tunes and setting verses to them.

DEVOUTLY RELIGIOUS

Henry was a surprisingly devout Catholic and was familiar with many religious writings. This illustration, from Henry's own psalter (book of psalms) shows the king reading liturgical texts, some of which he set to music.

COURTLY MUSIC

Professional musicians were employed to entertain the king at court and accompany him on his travels. Musicians nearly always performed in private, seldom at public functions, except dances. This lute, an early forerunner of the guitar, and flute are typical Tudor instruments.

A MAN OF LETTERS

Henry was an accomplished scholar, though he found writing somewhat tedious. He dictated most of his official letters, but his private correspondence, and his poetry, he wrote himself. His personal writing box is shown here, decorated with the royal coat-of-arms. It was made in 1525 of painted wood and gilt leather.

AN ACCOMPLISHED MUSICIAN

Henry was himself an accomplished musician and is reputed to have had a good singing voice. He is also credited with writing a number of songs, including 'Pastance With Good Company' and possibly the words to 'Greensleeves'.

AN AVID READER

Henry was an avid reader and could converse in English, Spanish, French and Latin. He encouraged others to read and insisted that his children were well-versed in the art at an early age.

VIRTUOSO PERFORMANCE

Women were allowed few privileges at court, though Henry allowed any who were accomplished musicians to give private recitals. The woman in this picture is playing an early form of fiddle; note the shape of the bow.

EVENTS OF HENRY'S LIFE

~1527 22ND JUNE~
Henry starts divorce against Catherine of Aragon

~1528~
Cardinal Wolsey gives Hampton Court to Henry

~1529 18TH JUNE~
Catherine of Aragon starts her defence

~1530 29TH NOVEMBER~
Wolsey arrested, later dies

~1532~
Archbishop Warham dies. Thomas Cranmer becomes Archbishop of Canterbury. Act of Succession passed

~17TH MAY~
Thomas More resigns as Chancellor

BREAK WITH THE CHURCH OF ROME

HENRY DEFIES THE POPE

This contemporary woodcut (c.1538) depicting the Pope as an antichrist, shows Henry defying papal power. It is typical of the anti-Catholic feeling that swept Europe in the 16th century.

There was already a growing body of people who objected to, and protested against corruption within the Catholic Church. They came to be known as Protestants and seized upon the opportunity to establish a new church in England by siding with the king. When the Pope refused to annul his marriage to Catherine of Aragon, Henry determined to take away the power of the clergy by Act of Parliament. Henry remained a Catholic throughout his life. The conversion of the Church of England to Protestantism came later, in Elizabeth I's reign.

THE REFORMATION

In 1533 Parliament passed the Act of Appeals, asserting England's independence from Rome. The following year the Act of Supremacy made Henry 'Supreme Head of the Church of England'.

THE ARREST OF THOMAS MORE

Sir Thomas More, Lord Chancellor and chief minister at the time, was a devout Catholic and refused to acknowledge Henry as head of the English Church. He was arrested and executed in 1535.

DEFENDER OF THE FAITH

Ironically, in 1521 Henry wrote a book defending the Catholic faith against the Protestant writings of Martin Luther, earning him the title 'Defender of the Faith' from the Pope. The abbreviation F.D. still appears on coins today.

EVENTS OF HENRY'S LIFE

~1533~
Act of Appeals passed

~25TH JANUARY~
Henry secretly marries Anne Boleyn

WILLIAM WARHAM

Archbishop of Canterbury from 1504 to 1532, Warham had officiated at the marriage of Henry and Catherine. He fought against Henry's break with the Church of Rome all his life.

DEFENDING THE REALM

CANNON FIRE

Detail of a bronze demi cannon, found aboard the *Mary Rose.* All Henry's guns carried the royal device of a rose in relief.

*H*enry VIII was a flamboyant and ambitious man, personally and politically. He took part in several military campaigns to strengthen his position in Europe, with varying degrees of success. Charles V of Spain, and Holy Roman Emperor, was also Catherine of Aragon's nephew and had already successfully attacked Rome, making the Pope politically subject to him. When Henry later sought permission of the Pope to divorce Catherine he was never likely to be received favourably. Following Henry's split with the Church of Rome, he spent the last years of his reign under threat of invasion to re-establish papal authority. In response, Henry built a chain of fortifications to protect the south coast.

THE ENGLISH NAVY

Although founded by his father, it was Henry VIII who first developed the navy into a proper fighting force. By the end of his reign the fleet was 80 strong.

HENRY'S SOUTH COAST FORTIFICATIONS

This map shows the distribution of Henry's castle-building programme along the south coast, always vulnerable to attack from Spain and France. The defences were mostly built between 1538-40 with money and materials from the recently closed monasteries.

BASTIONS OF DEFENCE

Deal Castle, Kent, as it appeared when newly completed in 1540. The largest of the Henrician coastal forts, it was also the most powerful, defended by cannons and handguns in three tiers of heavy bastions.

St. Ives
Falmouth
Plymouth Citadel
Paignton Torquay
Teignmouth
Exmouth
Falmouth
Sidmouth
Plymouth
Dartmouth
St. Mawes
Pendennis

FORTRESS PALACE

The only royal palace to be heavily fortified, the Tower of London, dating from Norman times, was a formidable fortress guarding Henry's capital city.

MEN-AT-ARMS

Tudor soldiers were only lightly armoured with helmets and breastplates (similar to this illustration). They were expected to provide their own weapons, which might be pistols, muskets, pikestaffs, or even crossbows.

EVENTS OF HENRY'S LIFE

~1533 23RD MAY~
Henry 'officially' divorces Catherine of Aragon

~7TH SEPTEMBER~
Princess Elizabeth born

~1534~
Act of Supremacy passed

~12TH APRIL~
Maid of Kent executed

~1535 22ND JUNE~
Bishop John Fisher executed

~6TH JULY~
Thomas More executed

ANNE BOLEYN

BORN
1502

MARRIED
1533

DIVORCED
1536

EXECUTED
1536

*W*hen it became clear that Catherine was not going to bear Henry a son, he began to lose interest in her, especially as the queen's looks began to fade. He had a series of mistresses, amongst whom was Anne Boleyn. He developed a genuine love for her and they married, in secret, probably on 25th January 1533, four months before his divorce from Catherine was finalised. Having failed, like Catherine, to deliver the king a son and heir, Henry resolved to end his second marriage. He began to tire of Anne and accused her of adultery with, amongst others, her own brother George, and of plotting to murder him. One of the accused confessed under torture, condemning them all to death. For some reason Henry had the marriage annulled two days before her execution on 19th May 1536.

SIGN OF THE TIMES

The date of Anne's birth is unknown, but is usually given as 1502. Not a classically beautiful woman, she had six fingers on one hand, which Henry cited against her in the divorce as a sign of witchcraft.

WAITING TO DIE

On 24th April 1536 Anne's own uncle, the Duke of Norfolk, was appointed by Thomas Cromwell to gather evidence against her. Whilst imprisoned in the Tower of London she etched her signature into the wall of her cell.

THE FUTURE QUEEN

Anne gave birth to Elizabeth on 7th September 1533, just eight months after her 'official' marriage to Henry. Elizabeth was a great disappointment to Henry, but eventually became queen in 1558.

ANNE'S JEWEL BOX

Amongst Anne's most treasured possessions was her jewellery, which she carried in this charming casket on her frequent processions between royal palaces. It is on display at Leeds Castle, Kent, one of her favourite homes.

CHILDHOOD HOME

Henry courted Anne at Hever Castle, Kent, her family home, built in 1340 and extended by her father, Sir Thomas Bullen (or Boleyn). Her ghost is said to haunt the gardens of Hever each Christmas.

EXECUTIONER'S SWORD

Anne was taken to the scaffold on Tower Green a little before noon, wearing a robe of black damask. An executioner, skilled in the use of the sword, was brought over specially from France, at her request. A sword similar to this may have been used.

MARY BOLEYN

Mary Boleyn, Anne's elder sister, became Henry's mistress in 1521 and is rumoured to have borne him a son. Anne was made Queen Catherine's lady-in-waiting and soon aroused the king's interest in place of Mary.

THE ROYAL PALACES

TUDOR KITCHENS

The kitchens at
Hampton Court
are still very much
as they were in
Henry's day.

enry VIII spent a vast fortune on
his royal residences, embellishing
existing palaces and building some
entirely new ones on a scale
unprecedented by any other English monarch.
He was determined to make an outward display
of his wealth and power to all the figureheads of
Europe. Henry's household regularly visited each
of the palaces at different times of the year.

HAMPTON COURT PALACE

Hampton Court began as a small medieval manor, belonging to the Knights Hospitallers, a religious order. Greatly extended by Wolsey into a palace, he was forced to give it to Henry in 1528, who embellished it still further.

NONSUCH PALACE

GREENWICH PALACE

The Tudor palace of Placentia, birthplace of Henry VIII and Elizabeth I, stood by the Thames at Greenwich, then just a village outside London. It was a magnificent medieval palace, greatly extended by Henry, and was his favourite residence. Although rebuilt by Charles II to designs by Wren, this view by Canaletto (c.1750) of the buildings (later converted for use as a naval hospital, college and maritime museum) still give a good idea of the grandeur of the riverside setting.

In 1538 Henry began his most ambitious building project, the Palace of Nonsuch, in Surrey. It was to be the most magnificent palace in Europe, but was never completed. Today, all trace of it has gone.

JANE SEYMOUR

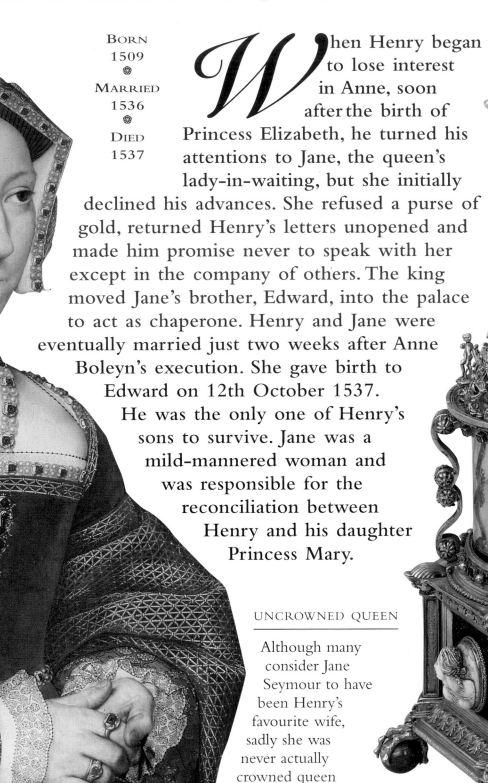

BORN
1509

MARRIED
1536

DIED
1537

When Henry began to lose interest in Anne, soon after the birth of Princess Elizabeth, he turned his attentions to Jane, the queen's lady-in-waiting, but she initially declined his advances. She refused a purse of gold, returned Henry's letters unopened and made him promise never to speak with her except in the company of others. The king moved Jane's brother, Edward, into the palace to act as chaperone. Henry and Jane were eventually married just two weeks after Anne Boleyn's execution. She gave birth to Edward on 12th October 1537. He was the only one of Henry's sons to survive. Jane was a mild-mannered woman and was responsible for the reconciliation between Henry and his daughter Princess Mary.

UNCROWNED QUEEN

Although many consider Jane Seymour to have been Henry's favourite wife, sadly she was never actually crowned queen before her untimely death on 24th October 1537.

THE FUTURE KING

As a young child Edward was intelligent and quite robust, but he was later struck down by a succession of illnesses. In January 1553 he contracted tuberculosis and died six months later, just 15 years old. He was the first king to be crowned as 'Supreme Head of the English Church'.

SALT OF THE EARTH

In medieval and Tudor times salt was considered a very expensive and important commodity, essential for the preservation of food. When Francis I, King of France, presented this combined clock and salt cellar, made of exquisitely wrought silver gilt, to Henry it would have been considered a fine gift.

THE QUEEN DIES

Jane had a prolonged labour with Edward, finally giving birth by Caesarean section, the surgeons using implements similar to these. Complications set in and she died of blood poisoning two weeks later.

EVENTS OF HENRY'S LIFE

~1536~
Dissolution of monasteries begins

~7TH JANUARY~
Catherine of Aragon dies

~17TH MAY~
Henry divorces Anne Boleyn

THE KING MOURNS

Henry is said to have really loved Jane and was distraught when she died following the birth of Edward. Her body was laid to rest at Windsor, where he himself was later buried. She is the only wife to share his grave.

EUROPEAN RELATIONS

WRESTLING

Henry VIII loved to wrestle, but he was thrown to the floor by Francis I in their friendly contest.

When Henry came to the throne England was still considered a minor player on the European political stage. Being a proud and arrogant man, he was keen to show his prowess on the battlefield and took part in several minor campaigns, with mixed results. In 1513 he joined forces with the Emperor Maximilian against France. When Wolsey's contrivances to hold the balance of power in Europe failed, it left Henry alone and humiliated. Wolsey was arrested in 1530 but died en-route to the Tower.

THE FIELD OF THE CLOTH OF GOLD (1520)

Following several years of wars, an uneasy peace prevailed in which
Henry briefly held the balance of power between France and
Spain. Wolsey organised a meeting, full of pomp and pageantry,
with Francis I (of France) outside Calais to try and bring about a
permanent alliance. No expense was spared by Henry. A small
'town' of tents and pavilions was set up to house the two kings and
their retainers. Henry wore a gold cloak and the meeting came to
be known as 'The Field of the Cloth of Gold'.

SIEGE OF BOULOGNE

This woodcut
shows Henry's army
laying siege to
Boulogne in 1544,
in a later campaign.
Powerful cannons
break through the
walls, while armed
knights await the
opportunity to
rout the city.

THOMAS WOLSEY (1475-1530)

Cardinal Wolsey, although
of humble birth, was made
Chancellor by Henry in 1514.
He was a powerful
politician who
virtually governed
the country
single-handedly
for 15 years,
until he fell from
favour in 1529.

EVENTS OF HENRY'S LIFE

~1536 19TH MAY~
Henry executes
Anne Boleyn

~MAY~
Henry marries
Jane Seymour

~8TH OCTOBER~
Pilgrimage of
Grace begins

~1537 FEBRUARY~
Robert Aske
executed

~12TH
OCTOBER~
Prince
Edward
born

DISSOLUTION OF THE MONASTERIES

'PILGRIMS OF GRACE'

Robert Aske led a pilgrimage from Yorkshire to London to demand that Henry reopen the monasteries. They disbanded peaceably but Henry treacherously executed Aske and many of his followers.

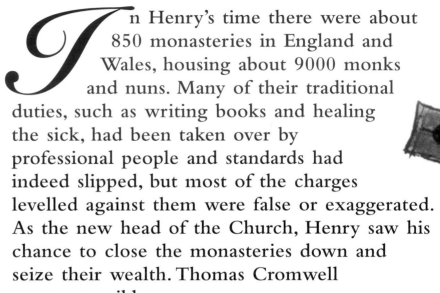

In Henry's time there were about 850 monasteries in England and Wales, housing about 9000 monks and nuns. Many of their traditional duties, such as writing books and healing the sick, had been taken over by professional people and standards had indeed slipped, but most of the charges levelled against them were false or exaggerated. As the new head of the Church, Henry saw his chance to close the monasteries down and seize their wealth. Thomas Cromwell was responsible for 'dissolving', or closing the monasteries between 1536-40.

REUSED STONE

In addition to topping up Henry's coffers by claiming their lands and riches, the monasteries also served as convenient quarries for stone in his castle-building programme, as shown left.

A TYPICAL DAY IN A MONASTERY	
Midnight	Matins (church service)
1am	Retire to bed
5am	Prime (church service)
6am	Breakfast
7am	Work duties
9am	Chapter Mass (church service)
10am	Meeting with abbot
11am	High Mass (church service)
12 noon	Dinner
1pm	Rest in dormitory
2pm	Work duties
4pm	Vespers (church service)
5pm	Work duties
6pm	Supper
7pm	Evening Prayer
8pm	Retire to bed

PENALTY FOR RESISTANCE

Cromwell's officials visited each monastery and requested that the brethren close it down voluntarily, forfeiting all their land and possessions to the king. Most complied, but if they refused they faced imprisonment, torture and possible execution, usually on trumped-up charges.

FALLEN FROM GRACE

One of the largely unproven charges levelled against the monasteries was that the monks and nuns had sunken into debauchery, spending their time drinking and fraternising instead of in quiet prayer.

AFTER THE DISSOLUTION

Many of the richer monasteries were sold or let to the king's favourites, who might convert them into fine houses. Others, like Bayham Abbey, Sussex, were stripped of their riches and left to slowly fall into ruins.

EVENTS OF HENRY'S LIFE

~1540 28TH JULY~
Henry marries
Catherine Howard

~1542~
Battle of Solway Moss

~13TH FEBRUARY~
Catherine Howard
executed

~1543 12TH JULY~
Henry marries
Catherine Parr

~1544 18TH
SEPTEMBER~
Siege of
Boulogne

~1545
19TH JULY~
*Mary
Rose
sinks*

ANNE OF CLEVES

BORN
1515

❖

MARRIED
1540

❖

DIVORCED
1540

❖

DIED
1557

*H*enry seems to have genuinely grieved for Jane Seymour and did not remarry for over two years following her death. Until then, Henry had married the women of his own choice, unusual for the monarchy who usually married for the benefits of political alliance. Thomas Cromwell and several other of the king's ministers were becoming increasingly concerned about Henry's role in Europe and were keen for the king to make a marriage of alliance to strengthen his position. Charles V of Spain and Francis I were mustering an army against England, threatening to re-establish papal power, so Henry desperately needed an ally in Europe. Somewhat reluctantly, he agreed to a political marriage of convenience, even though the threat of invasion passed.

IMMEDIATE DIVORCE

The marriage was never consummated and Henry sought an immediate divorce, which was granted six months later.

MATCHMAKER

Thomas Cromwell, Henry's current chief minister, was entrusted with the task of finding the king a new wife. A convenient political alliance between England and Germany might be formed if he could persuade Henry to marry one of the Duke of Cleves' sisters.

A COMFORTABLE RETIREMENT

Henry and Anne were a disappointment to one another from the start. She could speak no English and had few social graces. Educated more in domestic skills than in art, literature and music, all of which Henry loved, Anne retired to Richmond Palace, where she lived peaceably until her death in 1557.

THE 'FLANDERS MARE'

Holbein was sent to Germany to paint portraits of Anne and her sister Amelia. Henry chose Anne and agreed to marry her on the strength of it, but was later very disappointed with her, calling her the 'Flanders Mare'.

EVENTS OF HENRY'S LIFE

~1537 24TH OCTOBER~
Jane Seymour dies

~1538~
Henry builds
Nonsuch Palace

~1540~
Last monastery
closes

~6TH JANUARY~
Henry
marries Anne
of Cleves

~JULY~
Thomas
Cromwell
executed

~12TH JULY~
Henry divorces Anne
of Cleves

RESTLESS SPIRIT

Like Anne Boleyn, her cousin, also executed by Henry, Catherine Howard's spirit seems unable to rest. Her ghost is said to haunt this gallery at Hampton Court Palace.

UNSEEMLY BEHAVIOUR

Catherine was accused of adultery and conduct unbecoming a queen by Archbishop Cranmer. She was tried and found guilty, and later beheaded on 13th February 1542.

CATHERINE HOWARD

BORN
1521

MARRIED
1540

EXECUTED
1542

Catherine Howard became another pawn in the power struggles of Henry's court. Henry's marriage to Anne of Cleves had been a disaster and he soon began to look for a new bride. Anne's charming lady-in-waiting, Catherine Howard, soon caught his attention. Thomas Cromwell had strongly supported the king's marriage to Anne and his enemies were quick to encourage Henry to divorce her and marry Catherine as a means of ousting him from power. They married on 28th July 1540 just 16 days after Henry's divorce.

FLIRTATIOUS NATURE

Catherine Howard was the niece of the Duke of Norfolk. She became lady-in-waiting to Anne of Cleves at just 19. She was high spirited and quite uninhibited which, tragically for her, aroused the interest of the king.

THE QUEEN'S LAST JOURNEY

This is the last view Catherine Howard would have seen, before her imprisonment, as she approached the Traitor's Gate at the Tower of London. Her only real crime was in having a flirtatious nature, for which she paid with her life.

CATHERINE PARR

BORN
1512

MARRIED
1543

DIED
1548

Catherine Parr was the daughter of a minor noble, Sir Thomas Parr, who had risen through the ranks of Henry's court to become Controller of the Royal Household. Very little is known about Catherine's early life, or her courtship with Henry. A mature woman of 31 when she married Henry on 12th July 1543, she was already twice widowed. Well educated, she brought a sense of calm and dignity to the royal court. Henry was by now suffering from many ailments and Catherine nursed him in his final years. She supervised Edward's education and reconciled Mary and Elizabeth with Henry.

PRESENT FROM AN EMPEROR

This grotesque parade helmet was given to Henry by the Emperor Maximilian I in about 1514. By the time he married Catherine Parr his face had become so bloated the helmet no longer fitted.

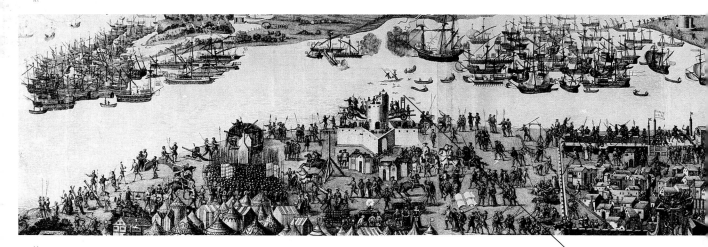

INSPECTING THE FLEET

Henry visited Portsmouth in July 1545 to inspect his navy in Southampton Water. He watched, humiliated, as the *Mary Rose* sank before his eyes.

This is where the *Mary Rose* sank, which is marked in the picture by floating bodies.

THE *MARY ROSE*

Henry's flagship, the *Mary Rose* (built in 1509), sank in the Solent on 19th July 1545. It was the first ship to be fitted with broadside-firing guns.

THE KING'S GREAT BED

Henry slept alone in the last years of his life in a bed similar to this one and had become so gross and overweight that he had to be hoisted into and out of bed by ropes and pulleys.

RELICS OF THE PAST

This fine collection of pewter plates was recovered from the *Mary Rose*. The wreck, and many artefacts of everyday life in Tudor times, are now on display in Portsmouth Historic Dockyard

THE QUEEN LIVES!

Catherine Parr outlived Henry, even though she was unable to bear him any children. A little while after the king's death she married Thomas Seymour, but died in 1548 after giving birth to a girl.

EVENTS OF HENRY'S LIFE

~1546 30TH DECEMBER~
Henry makes last will

~1547 28TH JANUARY~
Henry VIII dies

~20TH FEBRUARY~
Edward VI crowned

~1548~
Catherine Parr dies

~1553 6TH JULY~
Edward VI dies.
Mary I crowned

THE FADING YEARS

LAST WILL

Henry's will, dated 30th December 1546, settled succession first to Edward, then Mary, then Elizabeth when he died.

The sad, lonely figure that Henry had become by 1547 was a far cry from the strapping, athletic young man who ascended the throne some 38 years before. Always prone to severe headaches, which caused him to rage frequently, he also suffered bouts of smallpox and malaria. Both his legs were severely ulcerated, whether as a result of syphilis (probably also responsible for his fertility problems), varicose veins, which thrombosed, or osteomyelitis (a chronic infection, possibly caused by a jousting accident) is uncertain. The ulcers turned gangrenous and the smell of rotting flesh accompanied him in his final years. When Henry died on 28th January 1547 at St. James's Palace, few mourned the passing of his reign of tyranny.

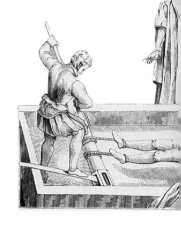

REIGN OF A TYRANT

Towards the end of his reign, Henry became more and more tyrannical in removing from office anyone who opposed him. Many thousands were tortured or executed by his order.

PRIVATE HEALTH CARE

In the final years of his life Henry required constant medical attention. This instrument case, decorated with the royal arms, belonged to his personal barber surgeon.

POWER STRUGGLE

John Dudley, Duke of Northumberland, one of the Council of Regency appointed by Henry to govern during Edward's minority. He later schemed to place Lady Jane Grey, his daughter-in-law, on the throne instead of Mary.

SAFETY FIRST

The king became obsessed with his personal safety in later life. He carried his own private lock when travelling, which he attached to his bed chamber door. Whilst staying at Allington Castle he went so far as to have himself walled-in each night!

EVENTS OF HENRY'S LIFE

~1557~
Anne of Cleves dies

~1558 17TH NOVEMBER~
Mary I dies.
Elizabeth I crowned
(last Tudor).

A WEIGHT PROBLEM

By the end of his life Henry had become quite obese and disfigured by illness. He had to be carried everywhere by servants and lifted up and down stairs with a hoist.

THE YOUNG ELIZABETH

RECONCILED

When Henry VIII died in 1547 Elizabeth was just 13 years old. The king had mostly ignored her but, thanks to the efforts of Catherine Parr, Henry's last wife, she was reconciled with her father in the last few years of his life.

Throughout her life Elizabeth put great store by being 'mere English', unlike her half-sister, Mary, whose mother, Catherine of Aragon, was Spanish. It was probably why she was so popular with her people, giving them a sense of national pride in a world dominated by Spain. Elizabeth never left English shores, not even to visit Wales, ancestral home of the Tudor dynasty.

IMPRISONED IN THE TOWER

In 1554 Elizabeth was imprisoned in the Tower of London because of her suspected involvement in Sir Thomas Wyatt's rebellion against Mary I's marriage to Philip of Spain.

The dates given in this book are in accordance with the Julian calendar, still being used at the time in England,

TRAGIC MOTHER

When Henry VIII's first wife, Catherine of Aragon, proved unable to bear him a son, the king took many mistresses, among whom was Anne Boleyn. They married, in secret, in January 1533, when Anne was already with child. Henry was gravely disappointed that Elizabeth was not the son he so desperately wanted as an heir and had little more to do with the young princess. He also soon tired of Anne and accused her of adultery, a 'crime' for which she was later executed in 1536.

VIRTUAL PRISONER

Elizabeth was an elegant, rather than a beautiful woman, of slim build with a fiery shock of red hair. She spent much of her early life a virtual prisoner, confined to several royal palaces, which probably accounts for her studious nature.

EVENTS OF ELIZABETH'S LIFE

~1491~
Henry VIII born
(Elizabeth's father)

~1502~
Anne Boleyn born
(Elizabeth's mother)

~1516~
Princess Mary born
(later Mary I)

~1533~
Henry VIII & Anne Boleyn marry.
Princess Elizabeth born (later Elizabeth I).
Act of Appeals asserts England's independence from Rome

CHILDHOOD HOME

Elizabeth was born at Greenwich Palace on 7th September 1533. She was taken soon after birth to Hatfield House, Hertfordshire, where she spent most of her early life.

AN EXCEPTIONAL PUPIL

Roger Ascham was appointed as Elizabeth's private tutor. She was his brightest pupil and displayed an exceptional flair for languages.

which was 10 days behind the Gregorian calendar, used by the Spanish since 1582 and now in universal use.

THE PATH TO THE THRONE

A QUEEN FOR NINE DAYS

Edward VI conferred the throne on his cousin, and childhood sweetheart, Lady Jane Grey. She ruled for just nine days before relinquishing the crown to Mary, Edward's half-sister, and was afterwards executed for treason.

Like her father, Henry VIII, Elizabeth was not born to rule and could never have expected to succeed to the throne. She was third in line after her half-brother Edward and half-sister Mary. Henry had several illegitimate children, including a son, Henry Fitzroy, by his mistress Elizabeth Blount in 1519. The king created him Duke of Richmond in 1525 and began grooming him for the throne. It was only after his untimely death in 1536 that Elizabeth was even considered a possible heir.

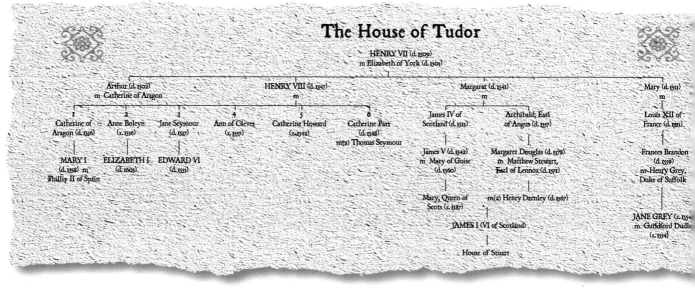

The House of Tudor

HENRY VII (d. 1509)
m Elizabeth of York (d. 1503)

Arthur (d. 1502)　　　　HENRY VIII (d. 1547)　　　　Margaret (d. 1541)　　　　Mary (d. 1533)
m Catherine of Aragon　　　　m　　　　　　　　　　m　　　　　　　　　　m

1　　　2　　　3　　　4　　　5　　　6
Catherine of　Anne Boleyn　Jane Seymour　Ann of Cleves　Catherine Howard　Catherine Parr
Aragon (d. 1536)　(x. 1536)　(d. 1537)　(x. 1557)　(x. 1542)　(d. 1548)
　　　　　　　　　　　　　　　　　　　　　　　mt(2) Thomas Seymour

James IV of　　　Archibald, Earl　　　Louis XII of
Scotland (d. 1513)　of Angus (d. 1557)　France (d. 1515)

MARY I　ELIZABETH I　EDWARD VI
(d. 1558) m　(d. 1603)　(d. 1553)
Phillip II of Spain

James V (d. 1542)　Margaret Douglas (d. 1578)　Frances Brandon
m Mary of Guise　m Matthew Stewart,　(d. 1559)
(d. 1560)　Earl of Lennox (d. 1571)　m Henry Grey,
　　　　　　　　　　　　Duke of Suffolk

Mary, Queen of　m(2) Henry Darnley (d. 1567)
Scots (x. 1587)

　　　　　　　　　　　　　　　　JANE GREY (x. 1554)
　　　　　　　　　　　　　　　　m Guildford Dudley
JAMES I (VI of Scotland)　　　　　　　　　(x. 1554)

House of Stuart

FAMILY TREE

Family Tree showing Elizabeth's path to the throne and her relationship to Edward and Mary.
All three of Henry's surviving children were born to different wives.

BOY KING

Edward VI succeeded to the throne in 1547, aged just nine, as Henry's only surviving legitimate male heir.

EVENTS OF ELIZABETH'S LIFE

~1533~
Henry VIII excommunicated by the Pope

~1534~
Act of Supremacy makes the monarch Supreme Head of the new Church of England

~1536~
Henry VIII divorces and executes Anne Boleyn. Duke of Richmond dies (Elizabeth's illegitimate half-brother)

~1537~
Prince Edward born (later Edward VI)

~1541~
Francis Drake born

~1547~
Henry VIII dies. Edward VI crowned

THE *LIBER REGALIS* OR CORONATION BOOK

Made in 1382 this book is believed to have been used at every coronation from Henry IV to Elizabeth I. Like many others of the time, Elizabeth put great store in astrology and ordered the astrologer John Dee to choose the most advantageous day for her coronation service. So it was that, although she ascended the throne on 17th November 1558, Elizabeth was not crowned until 15th January 1559.

THE KING'S DYING WISH

This anti-papal painting of Henry VIII's deathbed shows the king pointing to Edward as his successor. According to Henry's last will, dated 30th December 1546, succession was to pass first to Mary, then Elizabeth, should anything happen to his son.

FAMILY MATTERS

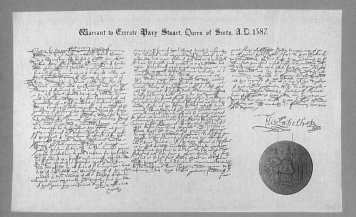

Warrant to Execute Mary Stuart, Queen of Scots. A.D. 1587.

A TRAGIC END

Aware that Mary had herself been used as a pawn in the political struggle for power, Elizabeth was reluctant to sign her death warrant. After 19 years of imprisonment, she was finally executed in 1587.

*E*lizabeth succeeded to the throne at 25 years of age amidst political and religious upheaval. Not least of her problems were the intrigues going on within her own family in an attempt to place a Catholic back on the throne of England. Her cousin Mary, Queen of Scotland in her own right and Elizabeth's closest relative, became embroiled in a plot (almost certainly against her will) to place her on the English throne. Elizabeth, for her part, tried to ensure the line of succession remained in Protestant hands by persuading Mary to marry one of her own favourites.

MARY TAKES FLIGHT

David Rizzio was murdered in front of Mary, Queen of Scots, in 1566. He was Mary's private secretary and was suspected of being her lover. Her husband, Henry Darnley, was implicated in the plot and a year later he himself was murdered. The following year, suspected of involvement in Darnley's death, she fled to England in exile.

SECRET LIAISONS

There were many suitors for Elizabeth's hand in marriage, the most notable being Robert Dudley, who lived at Kenilworth Castle. But he was already married to Amy Robsart. Amy tragically broke her neck amidst mysterious circumstances, implicating both Elizabeth and Dudley. To avoid further suspicion, perhaps, they did not marry. Instead, Elizabeth tried, unsuccessfully, to marry him off to her Catholic cousin, Mary, Queen of Scots. Instead, Mary married Lord Darnley, a Catholic.

These two views of Kenilworth Castle, in Warwickshire, show: the castle as it appears today in ruins and, below, as it would have looked at the time of Elizabeth's visit in 1575.

THE ROYAL 'PROGRESSES'

Elizabeth frequently took her court on tours, or 'progresses', around the country. Courtiers considered it an honour to be included on the royal tour, even though the cost might bankrupt them. Her longest visit was with Robert Dudley, at Kenilworth, in 1575, when she stayed for 19 days, feasting, hunting and enjoying lavish entertainment.

ELIZABETHAN COURT

The Elizabethan court was more than just an occasion for socialising, though undoubtedly entertainment formed a very important part of proceedings. All of the important decisions of government were made at court. It was also the place where ambitious politicians jostled for power and sought the queen's favours. To be seen at court was essential for personal advancement. Elizabeth had several favourites during the course of her long reign, the most notable in later years being Robert Devereux, Earl of Essex, whom she seems to have genuinely loved. She is said to have been devastated when he betrayed her and she was forced to sign his execution warrant for treason in 1601.

HAND IN GLOVE

Elizabeth was proud of her beautiful hands and often wore elegant gloves to show them off.

YOUNG LOVE

Robert Devereux, 2nd Earl of Essex, was just 20 years old when the ageing Elizabeth first fell under his charms in 1587. Although 34 years his senior, the queen loved him dearly. She forgave his impetuosity and conferred many honours upon him. Their unlikely romance lasted 12 years.

RIGHT-HAND MAN

Sir William Cecil, Principal Secretary of State, was Elizabeth's right-hand man in all matters of government until his death in 1598. He accompanied her at court and on her many 'progresses'.

THE PRICE OF VANITY

Ladies at court had to wear tight corsets, with metal or wooden stays, beneath their clothes to make them look as slim as possible above the bustle of their long gowns. This unique garment belonged to Elizabeth and was used on her funeral effigy.

QUEEN OF THE DANCE

Life at Elizabeth's court was often a lively affair. She is seen here dancing with Robert Dudley, Earl of Leicester, who asked for, but was refused, her hand in marriage.

FRANKLYN'S CIGARETTES.

QUEEN ELIZABETH & SIR W. RALEIGH.

CHIVALROUS BEHAVIOUR

Sir Walter Raleigh was one of Elizabeth's great favourites. Though it is doubtful if he ever did spread his cloak before her, his behaviour was very chivalrous towards her.

EVENTS OF ELIZABETH'S LIFE

~1549~
Cranmer's English Prayer Book published

~1553~
Edward VI dies.
Mary I crowned.
Sir Hugh Willoughby leads expedition to find N.E. Passage

~1554~
Elizabeth imprisoned in Tower of London.
Mary I marries Philip of Spain.
Thomas Wyatt executed.
Lady Jane Grey executed

~1558~
Mary I dies

THE BEGINNINGS OF AN EMPIRE...

The Elizabethan period really was an age of adventure and discovery when, for the first time, English mariners, such as Drake, Willoughby and Frobisher, sailed beyond their immediate shores and explored the very limits of the known world. New trade routes were opened up between such places as North and South America, Russia, Persia and India. Merchants bought, or exchanged home-produced items for exotic goods, bringing untold wealth to Britain.

GIFT FROM A QUEEN

When Drake returned from his circumnavigation of the world, he gave Elizabeth a coconut as a memento. She had a magnificent silver cup made to encase it, which she afterwards presented to him in thanks.

CULINARY DELIGHTS

Several of the newly introduced herbs and spices were used for culinary purposes to disguise the often rancid taste of Elizabethan food.

FROM THE NEW WORLD

These American Indians, from Virginia, are eating maize, one of the many foods discovered in the 'New World'.

THE SPICE OF LIFE

Some of the spices imported
from the Americas, Asia and
the Middle East also had
medicinal properties,
such as nutmeg – used,
sparingly, for various
digestive disorders.

COLONY THAT FAILED

Sir Walter Raleigh established a new
colony in North America in 1584,
which he named Virginia, after
Elizabeth, the 'Virgin Queen', but its
initial success was short-lived and by
1590 it was deserted.

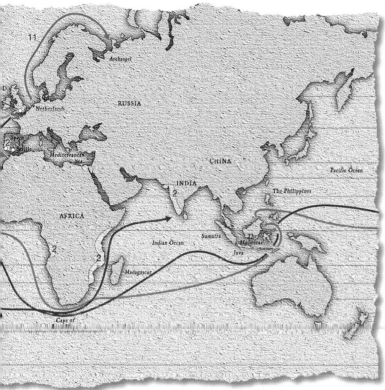

WORLD EXPLORATION

The map above shows the principal new trade
routes opened up by the Elizabethan explorers,
bringing cheap new goods to Britain from all
regions of the world.

DRESSING FOR DINNER

Chillies, peppers
and other exotic
foods introduced
from the Americas,
were used in cooking
as a flavouring, or
sprinkled on salads
as a condiment.

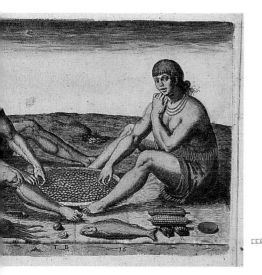

KILL OR CURE

Sir John Hawkins introduced
tobacco to England from
America (where the native
Indians smoked it in clay
pipes) in about 1565.
Originally, it was used as
a medicine to purge the
body of phlegm.

...THE BEGINNINGS OF AN EMPIRE

*T*he King of Spain, Philip II, had hoped to unite the throne of England and Spain by marrying Mary I, but his plans were foiled when she died in 1558. Instead, England became a thorn in his side. What had begun as a small group of privateers stealing Spain's wealth in a series of piratical raids, turned into a more serious quest for power. As England's naval commanders became ever more daring and proficient in their exploits, they posed a very real threat to the might of Spain. The colonies and trade routes they established were soon the foundation on which England, in later years, built her empire.

WORLD TOUR

Between 1577–80 Francis Drake completed his circumnavigation of the world, the first Englishman to do so. On his return, he became a national hero and was rewarded the following year by being knighted by Elizabeth aboard his ship, the *Golden Hind*.

PART-TIME NAVY

It was expensive to keep ships in constant service. When not required they were laid up in port and their crews paid off.

PRIDE OF THE FLEET

The '*Ark Royal*', shown here, was the flagship of the English navy. New designs by such shipwrights as Matthew Baker, made English ships much more manoeuvrable than those used by our enemies and played a key role in establishing England as a naval power.

RICHES FROM ABROAD

Elizabethan explorers brought back more than gold when they returned from distant parts of the globe. Merchants became extremely rich as the demand grew for new foodstuffs and materials from abroad.

'AT THE COURT OF QUEEN ELIZABETH....'

As Elizabeth's prestige and status grew throughout Europe, England came to be recognised as a growing world power. Many foreign ambassadors visited her at court to strike trade deals and negotiate political alliances to improve their country's position should England ever replace Spain as the dominant power in Europe. Here, she receives two Dutch officials in the Privy Chamber.

THE ARMADA ...

THE BUILD UP

E ver since Henry VIII's break with the Church of Rome, England had been under threat of invasion from the Catholic countries of Europe, especially after the Pope excommunicated Elizabeth in 1580. Spain was the most powerful country in Europe at that time and Philip II needed little persuasion to lead an invasion force against England, particularly as Elizabeth's navy openly inflicted acts of piracy on his fleet. In 1587 a council of war decided to launch a combined offensive against England. An armada of ships would be sent to the Netherlands, where they would collect a huge army and launch an offensive on the Kent coast, and afterwards march on London.

KEY

Catholic

Protestant

area of mixed

Othodox Christ and Islam

RELIGIOUS DIVISIONS

This map shows the political and religious divisions of Europe at the time of the Armada. By sending a force against England, Spain hoped to reunite Europe under Catholicism.

Lisbon

A LOVE SCORNED

Philip II, King of Spain, was Elizabeth's brother-in-law. In 1554 he had married Mary, her Catholic half-sister, and had offered his hand in marriage to Elizabeth soon after her succession, but she refused him.

EARLY WARNING SYSTEM

A system of beacons around the coast warned of the Armada's approach. Each beacon, within sight of its neighbours, could convey a warning the length of the country in minutes.

~1558~
Elizabeth ascends throne (last Tudor monarch). William Cecil created Secretary of State

~1559~
Elizabeth crowned. Elizabethan Prayer Book published

~1560~
Amy Robsart dies. Treaty of Edinburgh signed. Catholicism outlawed in Scotland

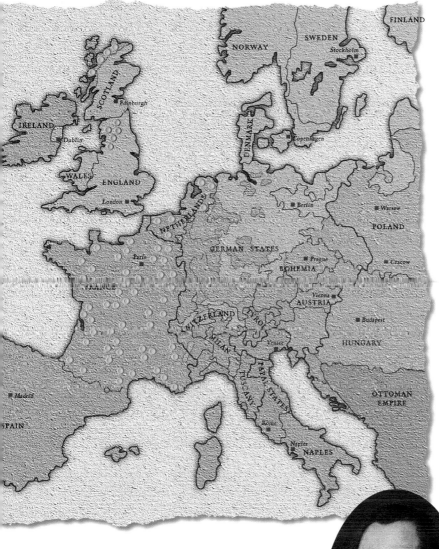

THE ROUTE OF THE ARMADA

The map above shows the route taken by the Armada. It set out from Lisbon on 20th May 1588 only to be scattered by bad weather. On 12th July, after revictualling and repairs, it set out again from La Coruna, in northern Spain, arriving in the Channel, off the Scilly Isles, on 19th July.

DRAKE ACQUIRES HIS SEA LEGS

Sir Francis Drake was born at Tavistock, Devon, in c.1541, though he learned his seafaring skills on the River Medway, in Kent, after his father, a naval chaplain, transferred to Chatham Dockyard around 1550.

...THE ARMADA

THE BATTLE COMMENCES

The Spanish Armada consisted of 138 ships in all, comprising 24 galleons, 40 merchantmen converted for war, 25 hulks to carry supplies and several other smaller vessels. By comparison, the English had 21 first-line ships and 40 of the second-line, with numerous support vessels, so the fleets were evenly matched. The English had an estimated 14,000 men compared with the Spanish total of about 24,000, but had 2000 cannons, nearly double the `Spanish number. The commander of the Spanish fleet was the Duke of Medina Sidonia. The English knew that the Spanish fleet was being amassed against them and tried to intersect it by launching a surprise attack before the Armada left Spanish waters. Unfortunately, bad weather foiled their plans and the English were driven back to port on the same day that the Spanish left La Coruna for the Channel.

THE BATTLE PLAN

This map shows how the course of the battle fared, from the first sighting of the Armada off the Lizard in Cornwall, to the final routing as a result of the havoc caused by the fireships off Calais.

THE ARMADA IS SIGHTED

According to unsubstantiated tradition, when Drake heard news at Plymouth that the Armada had been sighted, he insisted on finishing his game of bowls first.

RUNNING BATTLE

The English captains stole the advantage by performing several daring manoeuvres, but they were unable to strike at the heart of the Armada. A week-long running battle ensued as the prevailing wind carried the Armada towards its destination.

AN ILL WIND

Initially, it looked as if all would be lost when the prevailing wind and tide prevented most of the English fleet from leaving harbour. The skill of the English captains in managing to put to sea at all dismayed the Spanish.

FIRE IN THE NIGHT

The Armada successfully reached Calais and anchored, awaiting the arrival of their allies in Flanders. On the night of 28th July eight fireships, hulks laden with pitch and gunpowder, were set alight and cast adrift by the English amongst the Spanish fleet. The Spanish captains panicked and made for the open sea. Although the fireships did not actually set fire to any enemy ships, they succeeded in breaking their formation. This proved to be the turning point in the battle and the following day the scattered Armada was attacked mercilessly by the English. The Spanish fleet fled into the North Sea with the English in hot pursuit.

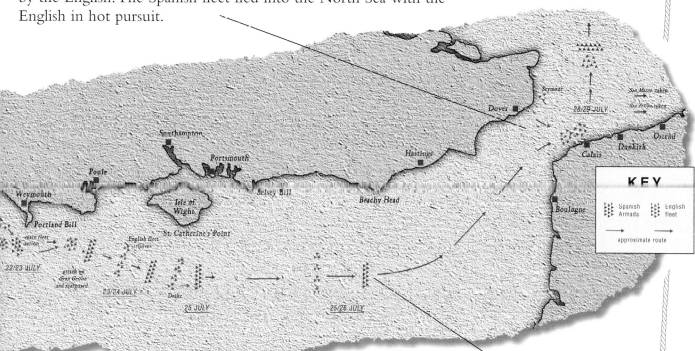

KEY

Spanish Armada

English fleet

approximate route

THE BATTLE RAGES

The Armada was formed into a crescent shaped formation and moved slowly up the Channel towards Calais. The first major engagement with the English fleet took place off Portland Bill, Dorset.

OUT-MANOEUVRED

Despite being out-manoeuvred by the English fleet, and suffering some losses, the Spanish maintained their tight formation and continued steadily up the Channel towards Calais.

...THE ARMADA

THE FLIGHT

A lthough the English had given a good account of themselves, the Armada succeeded in reaching its first objective, Calais, where they were to be joined by the Duke of Parma's army to invade England, but Dutch rebels prevented Parma's ships from putting to sea. Of the 138 ships that set out from Spain only 67 returned, most falling victim to the treacherous seas around Scotland and Ireland. The crews were ravaged by hunger and disease. Philip was devastated by the news that his grand plan had failed and, although in a few years his navy was stronger than ever, Spain never fully recovered from the humiliating defeat.

THE FLIGHT OF THE ARMADA

This map shows the route taken by the Armada in retreat. Prevailing winds aided their escape around the coasts of Scotland and Ireland. Howard pursued them for three days before returning home to victory celebrations.

COMMANDER OF THE FLEET

The queen's Catholic cousin, Lord Charles Howard of Effingham, was chosen to command the English fleet. Although not a professional sailor, he was a strong and able commander, which Elizabeth needed to keep her sometimes impetuous sea captains in check.

THE ARMADA JEWEL

This enamelled-gold jewel, set with diamonds and rubies, is said to have been given by Elizabeth to Sir Thomas Heneage, Vice-Chamberlain, after the defeat of the Armada.

HEARTS OF OAK

John Hawkins had the fighting vessels of the English navy rebuilt to bold new designs. Previously, ships were little more than floating fighting platforms, but the new ships were sleeker and equipped with many more guns, capable of firing broadside.

THE CHATHAM CHEST

Following the defeat of the Armada, Hawkins and Drake set up a voluntary fund for the support of distressed seamen, held at Chatham Dockyard in this chest.

DRAKE'S DRUM

When this drum was beaten aboard Drake's ship the men mustered for battle. After the defeat of the Armada, many legends sprang up around the drum, including one that says Drake will return from the grave to fight for England if ever it is beaten.

EVENTS OF ELIZABETH'S LIFE

~1562~
Elizabeth contracts smallpox and nearly dies

~1564~
William Shakespeare born

~1565~
Tobacco first introduced into England

Lord Darnley proclaimed King of Scotland; marries Mary

~1566~
David Rizzio murdered

~1567~
Lord Robert Darnley murdered

~1568~
Mary Queen of Scots flees to England in exile

~1571~
Elizabeth opens Royal Exchange

~1572~
John Knox, church reformer, dies. William Cecil becomes Lord High Chancellor. Massacre at St. Bartholomew, Paris

1575
Elizabeth stays at Kenilworth with Robert Dudley for 19 days

1576
Martin Frobisher attempts to find N.W. Passage

POLITICAL INTRIGUES

Somerviles haste to Kill the Queene.

TIT-FOR-TAT

The Catholic John Somerville plotted to shoot Elizabeth in 1583, but his plan failed and he committed suicide in the Tower. A Bond of Association was afterwards formed whereby if Elizabeth's life was again threatened, the imprisoned Mary Queen of Scots would be executed, whether she was involved or not.

Throughout her reign, Elizabeth was surrounded by political intrigue as her various courtiers jostled for position and power. Towards the end of her reign, Robert Devereux, Earl of Essex, became her 'favourite' and was sent to Ireland to solve the crisis developing there. The Irish often formed an uneasy alliance with Spain, making England vulnerable to attack from that quarter. Several attempts were made to colonise Ireland with Protestant settlers, but they met with the same stout resistance experienced by colonists in America. Because Elizabeth relied so heavily on privateers to attain her position of power, the way was clear for them to amass huge personal fortunes, especially as new trade routes were opened up around the world. A more than generous tax system allowed the rich to keep much of their wealth, but at the expense of the royal purse. The situation was made worse by the mounting cost of the ongoing wars with Spain and Ireland.

OPEN REVOLT IN IRELAND

In 1598 the Earl of Tyrone inflicted a humiliating defeat on the English at the 'Battle of the Yellow Ford', near Armagh. This sparked off a general uprising amongst the Irish and many Protestant settlers were put to death. Elizabeth blamed the defeat partly on Essex's mishandling of the situation.

THE COLONIES TAKE ROOT

While the opening of new trade routes was Elizabeth's primary concern, others favoured colonisation to establish a foothold in the New World. Richard Grenville, seen here surrendering to the Spanish in 1591, was foremost amongst these, though most of the early colonies failed.

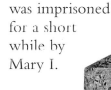

TRAITOR'S GATE

The old water gate, known as Traitor's Gate, is where water-borne prisoners were brought into the Tower of London to face imprisonment or execution, including Elizabeth herself when she was imprisoned for a short while by Mary I.

EVENTS OF ELIZABETH'S LIFE

~1577~
Drake sets out to circumnavigate the world

~1580~
Drake returns from his circumnavigation of the world. Elizabeth excommunicated by the Pope

~1581~
Drake knighted. Edmund Campion executed

~1583~
John Somerville attempts to assassinate Elizabeth

TRUSTED FRIENDS

The queen was constantly on her guard from assassination attempts, so she surrounded herself with trusted friends at all times, as shown in this procession.

AN AGE OF DISCOVERY

CENTRE OF THE UNIVERSE

Armillary spheres were used to demonstrate the movement of heavenly bodies. In Elizabeth's day, the other planets in the solar system were thought to revolve around the Earth, which was seen as the centre of the universe.

The journeys of Elizabethan explorers are all the more incredible because many of the seas they crossed were uncharted. They had little way of knowing if they would return from their voyages or perish in the attempt. Captains, such as Drake, were also extremely skilled and capable navigators and map-makers. The continuing war with Spain closed many of England's traditional trading routes in Europe, so the need to open up new ones in other parts of the world became more pressing. Elizabeth herself sponsored many of the voyages and is reputed to have made 4,000% profit on her original investment from Drake's circumnavigation of the world.

AFTERMATH OF THE ARMADA

The good old days experienced by English privateers, of attacking Spanish outposts and vessels, almost at will, were gone following the defeat of the Armada. Spanish defences improved radically and Drake's last expedition to Porto Rico failed. He died of dysentery in 1596 and was buried at sea off Porto Bello, in the Caribbean.

SEARCH FOR THE STARS

As journeys became more adventurous, and so more perilous, the need for more sophisticated equipment became more pressing. Mathematicians and astronomers throughout Europe turned their attentions towards developing more accurate navigational instruments, aided by information brought back by the explorers. A Polish astronomer, Nicolaus Copernicus, first suggested that the Earth rotated on its axis and orbited around the sun, an idea supported by John Dee, the queen's own astrologer and astronomer. He was also one of the foremost mathematicians of his time and carried out much pioneering work in calculating longitude by utilising the magnetic properties of lodestone.

EXOTIC FRUITS

The pineapple, a native fruit of Central and South America, was one of the many new plants brought back by the explorers. It quickly became a favourite delicacy at table.

NO SMOKE WITHOUT FIRE

Sir Walter Raleigh made smoking fashionable, though it was often regarded with suspicion. Here, his servant douses him with water, thinking him to be on fire.

STAPLE DIET

Potatoes were introduced from Virginia about 1596. Unlike other new foods, regarded with some suspicion, potatoes soon became accepted as part of the normal diet.

MERRIE ENGLAND

Sir Philip Sidney,
soldier, scholar,
writer and poet,
came to represent
the epitome of all
that was chivalrous
at Elizabeth's court.
He was mortally
wounded at the
Battle of Zutphen
and was given a
hero's funeral at
St. Paul's Cathedral,
an unprecedented
honour.

For most ordinary people the real benefit brought about by Elizabeth's strong reign was that of stability. The civil wars that had raged between Protestants and Catholics during Mary's turbulent reign were at an end and the country was restored to a period of relative calm and prosperity. Although little of the wealth generated by Elizabeth's merchant adventurers found its way down to peasant level, most people welcomed the sense of normality that had returned to their lives. Elizabeth had succeeded in uniting a divided country and a sense of national pride was felt by most people. For a while life was good, and there was much to celebrate and be grateful for.

VIRTUOSO

Elizabeth was
herself an
accomplished
musician
and could
play several
instruments.
The virginals (an early
type of harpsichord) shown
here bear the Boleyn family coat-of-arms.

FAMILY ENTERTAINMENT

Professional musicians were employed to entertain guests in large households. Most people from wealthy families were expected to play an instrument or be able to sing.

EVENTS OF ELIZABETH'S LIFE

~1584~
Walter Raleigh establishes a colony in Virginia

~1585~
Drake sacks Santiago

COUNTRY DANCING

Most people in Elizabethan times needed little excuse to celebrate. Country dances were a popular form of entertainment. The villagers here are dancing round a maypole as part of the May Day festivities.

TO BE OR NOT TO BE ...

Before Elizabeth's time most plays were performed by strolling players in the market place or inn yards. The first purpose-built theatres were erected in London in 1576. William Shakespeare was the most popular actor and dramatist of his day and often gave personal readings to the queen at court.

CHURCH MATTERS

THE ROOT OF ALL EVIL

Elizabeth was a very devout Christian and felt that strong religious belief held the key to good government and everyone's general well-being:
'One matter toucheth me so nearly as I may not overskip - religion, the ground on which all other matters ought to take root, and being corrupted, may marr the whole tree.'

The formation of the Church of England was something of a compromise, introduced by the opportunist Henry VIII, who merely took advantage of the growing tide of Protestantism sweeping across Europe to satisfy his personal ends. As long ago as the 14th century church reformers such as John Wycliffe had tried to introduce new ideas into Catholic doctrines. Catholics objected to any changes, while Protestant extremists felt the new Anglican Church did not go far enough, but it was generally welcomed when compared to the religious persecutions of Mary I's reign.

IN DEFIANCE OF ROME

Anti-Catholic feelings were rife throughout Europe in the 16th century. This woodcut shows the Pope as anti-Christ.

PERSECUTION

Witchcraft was still punishable by death and was not finally abolished as a crime until 1736.

THE WITCHES' SABBAT

Anyone who still practised the old pagan ways was generally termed a witch. However, many villages still tolerated a witch, or 'wise woman', in their midst, usually for their medical or fortune-telling abilities, even though witchcraft was illegal.

FIRST ARCHBISHOP

Matthew Parker was appointed Elizabeth's first Archbishop of Canterbury. He adopted a middle-of-the-road stance, rejecting the extreme religious views of both Catholic and Protestant, supporting the monarchy as head of the new Anglican Church.

FAMILY VALUES

Elizabethan families set great store by family values. The church instructed people to fear God and urged parents to teach the scriptures and encourage their children to say their prayers.

THE VIRGIN QUEEN

At the beginning of her reign Elizabeth is recorded as saying that she already considered herself to be married, to 'the Kingdom of England' and referred to her coronation ring as a symbol of that union. She was often referred to as 'Gloriana', the pure and beautiful maiden. Throughout her long reign, however, the queen had many suitors, any one of whom might have become her husband and given her an heir, but later on her political advisers positively encouraged her to remain a spinster. She had proved herself to be a strong-willed ruler, much-loved by her people, and many feared that she might lose that popularity if she married and were influenced by a husband less able than herself.

APPEARANCES CAN BE DECEPTIVE

The queen tried to hide her age, and the scars left by smallpox, in later years with the overuse of cosmetics. Her face and neck were heavily powdered and painted white, giving her a very pallid appearance.

PERSONAL HYGIENE

Elizabeth was quite fastidious for her day and took great care over her personal hygiene. She carried a pomander, filled with fragrant herbs and perfumes, to combat the often unpleasant smells encountered in Tudor households.

BUSINESS AS USUAL

The Royal Exchange, in London, built by the financier Sir Thomas Gresham and opened by the queen in 1571, was an outward sign of the growing prosperity of England during Elizabeth's reign. Rich merchants from home and abroad gathered there to conduct their business.

STRICT STANDARDS

One of the many standards introduced by Elizabeth to control unscrupulous merchants was this set of bronze weights, used as the official standard for all commercial weights.

YOUNG AT HEART

In later years the queen was said to be almost bald and wore a wig of thick red hair to appear more youthful. She had also lost many of her teeth, which impaired her speech.

THE END OF AN ERA

**LIFE TAKES
ITS TOLL**

This painting shows
Elizabeth on her
deathbed. By the
time she died the
queen was a tired
old woman. She
certainly suffered
from bouts of
depression towards
the end of her reign,
as she became
increasingly aware
perhaps that her
time of greatness
was nearly over.

In her last speech to parliament, known as the 'Golden Speech', Elizabeth, aware that her glorious time was nearly over, summed up her own reign thus: 'Though God has raised me high, yet this I count the glory of my crown - that I have reigned with your loves .... And though you have had, and may have, many princes more mighty and wise, sitting in this state, yet you never had, or shall have, any that will be more careful and loving.'

She knew the good times were over and troubles lay ahead, but she retained a sense of humility to the last. She was the first English monarch to give her name to an age.

**FALL FROM
GRACE**

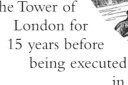

Sir Walter Raleigh,
one of Elizabeth's
favourites, fell
from favour under
James I. Convicted
on a trumped-up
charge of treason
in 1603, he was
imprisoned in
the Tower of
London for
15 years before
being executed
in 1618.

THE QUEEN'S SUCCESSOR

When Elizabeth died, childless,
in 1603, succession passed
to James Stuart, the
son of Mary
Queen of
Scots and
her closest
living
relative.

THE GOOD OLD DAYS

This effigy of Elizabeth
is from her tomb in
Westminster Abbey and
shows the queen as a
frail old lady. Her
glorious reign had
brought untold
wealth to England,
but by 1603 serious
problems loomed ahead.
Many of her trusted advisers
were dead, inflation soared
and the mounting cost of the
wars with Spain and Ireland
had left the exchequer
virtually bankrupt.

THE FINAL JOURNEY

Elizabeth died on 24th March 1603 at Richmond
Palace, from where her body was conveyed
by royal barge to Whitehall in preparation
for her funeral. This picture shows part
of the impressive funeral procession on
28th April, making its way to Westminster
Abbey, where an estimated 1600 mourners
waited to pay their last respects. Her coffin
was surmounted by an impressive effigy of
the queen in crown and full royal regalia.

INDEX

ACKNOWLEDGEMENTS

Picture Credits   t=top, b=bottom, c=centre, l=left, r=right
Abbreviation: BAL=Bridgeman Art Library

Ann Ronan at Image Select; 4cl, 12bl, 24bc, 25bl, 31bl, 35br, 36cr, 36/37c. Ashmolean Museum, Oxford; 70tl. Asprey & Co., London/BAL; 10c. Barnaby's Picture Library; 27l. Bodleian Library; 4tl/5c (Roll 156B. frame 9), 4bl (163C.7), 5b (156B.25), 6tl (263.3.3), 8b (263.3.4), 8/9t (156B.17), 9br (263.3.8), 9cr (165E.14), 9tr (163C.2), 11tl (156B.68), 12cl (156B.58), 14/15c (156B.64), 20/21ct (156B.78), 21b (209.10), 22tl (163C.12), 25tl (163C.16), 28tl (215.3.12), 28/29c (163C.15), 29tr (215.3.16), 31tl (209.9), 32tl (163C.17), (MS Ashmole 1758, fol.83v); 72/73cb. Board of Trustees of the National Museums and Galleries on Merseyside (Walker Art Gallery, Liverpool); 36bl. The Board of Trustees of the Royal Armouries; 34tl, 37c, 60tl. British Library, London/BAL; 40tl, 41ct, 57c, 88bl, 92b. British Museum, London/BAL; 16tl. Collection of the Earl of Derby, Suffolk/BAL; 15br.   Reproduced by courtesy of His Grace the Lord Archbishop of Canterbury - Copyright reserved to the Courtauld Institute of Art and the Church Commissioners - Photograph Courtauld Institute of Art; 89c. English Heritage Photographic Library; 44bl, 56cl, 68/69. E.T. Archive; 7tr, 11/12ct. Filkins, London/BAL; 9c. Fitzwilliam Museum, University of Cambridge/BAL; 11cr, 54/55ct. Fotomas Index; 25c, 48b, 88/89c. Glasgow Museums: The Stirling Maxwell Collection, Pollock House - A Sanchez Coello *Philip II*; 76l. Crown Copyright. Guildhall Art Gallery, Corporation of London/BAL; 25br, 69t. Hatfield House, Hertfordshire/BAL; 22bl. Hermitage, St. Petersburg/BAL; 12l. © Harrogate Museums and Art Gallery, North Yorkshire/BAL; 39tr. Heather Angel; 34/35cb. Hever Castle Ltd; 40/41c, 62/63ct. Hever Castle Ltd/BAL; 46l, 47br, 55cb. Historic Royal Palaces (Crown Copyright); 12r, 12c, 18bl, 52tl, 59tl, 59c, 82/83c. © Historic Scotland; 26tl. Hulton Deutsch Collection Ltd.; 22/23c, 38tr, 62tl, 65b. John Bethell/BAL; 52/53ct. Kremlin Museums, Moscow/BAL; 16/17b. Kunsthistorisches Museum, Vienna/BAL; 52l.© Leeds Castle Foundation; 11br, 28bl, 32cr, 33bl, 36/37ct, 38/39cb,39cl, 47tr. Manor House, Stanton Harcourt, Oxon/BAL; 29tl. The Mansell Collection; 57tl, 75t. Mary Evans Picture Library; 15cr, 22/23ct, 36/37b, 38l, 41br, 42tl, 42bl, 42cr, 44/45ct, 46/47cb, 51br, 53tr, 54bl, 56bl, 64tl,64c, 65tr, 66tl, 67tl, 68tl, 69b, 71c, 73tr, 74bl, 75br, 77tl, 78b, 79b, 81l, 82tl, 82bl, 83t, 84bl, 85tr, 85cr, 86/87c, 87tl, 87r, 89br, 91tl, 91br, 92tl, 92/93c. © Mary Rose Trust; 11cr, 11bl, 15bl, 40br, 41c, 42/43ct, 44tl, 60cr. Mittelalterliches Kriminalmuseum; 32bl. Museum of London; 20/21c, 24/25c. Museum of London/BAL; 6/7, 19t, 90cb, 90/91b. National Maritime Museum, London; 17tr, 20bl, 26/27c, 26bl, 30cl, 30/31c, 35ct, 45cr, 45r, 47tl, 52/53, 54cr, 64b, 67b, 78/79t, 80l, 80br, 84tl. By courtesy of the National Portrait Gallery, London; 67b, 70bl, 70r, 93tl. National Trust Photographic Library/Ian Shaw; 18c. Philip Mould, Historical Portraits Ltd., London/BAL; 23. Plymouth City Museums & Art Gallery collection; 81b. © Portsmouth City Council; 60b. Prado, Madrid/BAL; 25tr. Private Collection/BAL; 11tl, 58/59, 61tl, 83b, 88tl. Reproduced by kind permission of the President and Council of the Royal College of Surgeons of London; 20tl, 51c. Richard Kalina; 14/15ct. Royal Armouries; 29b. Tate Gallery, London; 11tr. The Mansell Collection;4/5t, 24br. The National Portrait Gallery, London; 15tr, 21cr, 27bl, 33r, 39br, 49br, 59tr, 61br, 61br.   The Royal Collection © Her Majesty The Queen; 49t. The Science Museum/Science & Society Picture Library; 30b, 31r. David Sellman; 47cl. Victoria & Albert Museum, London/BAL; 11cl, 34tr, 40bl, 48tl, 59t. 61c, 81t, 86b. Reproduced by permission of Viscount De L'Isle, from his private collection; 71t. The Worshipful Company of Barbers; 62bl. Worshipful Company of Goldsmiths; 50/51c. By Courtesy of the Dean and Chapter of Westminster; 66/67c, 71bl, 90tl, 93r.

A CIP Catalogue for this book is available from the British Library. ISBN 1 86007 636 X